I0456392

the HEALTHY ALPHABET

"This book brings you fun and educational learning by teaching you the alphabet and how to make healthy food choices!"

written by
MARK MCGINTY

illustrated by
JEFF WALPOLE

Disclaimer: The Healthy Alphabet is intended for educational and entertainment purposes only. The information and suggestions within this book, including references to foods, are not a substitute for professional medical advice, diagnosis, or treatment. Always consult a healthcare provider, nutritionist, or pediatrician before introducing new foods into your child's diet, especially if your child has allergies, intolerances, or other dietary restrictions. The authors, illustrators, and publishers do not assume any responsibility for any adverse effects or reactions that may result from the consumption of foods mentioned in this book or any related activities.

The Healthy Alphabet © 2024 Mark McGinty, Jeff Walpole
Illustrations © 2024 Jeff Walpole

Published by Pandamonium Publishing House www.pandamoniumpublishing.com

All rights reserved. No part of this book may be reproduced, stored in a retrieval system, or transmitted in any form or by any means, electronic, mechanical, photocopying, recording, or otherwise, without the prior written permission of the publisher, except in the case of brief quotations embodied in critical articles or reviews.

ISBN: 978-1-998467-07-5

Printed in Canada

A is for Apple! Apples are red, green and yellow and can keep your teeth healthy.

B is for **Broccoli!** Broccoli is green and gives your body and brain lots of nutrients.

C is for **Carrot!** Carrots are orange. Eating them can help make sure you have healthy eyes.

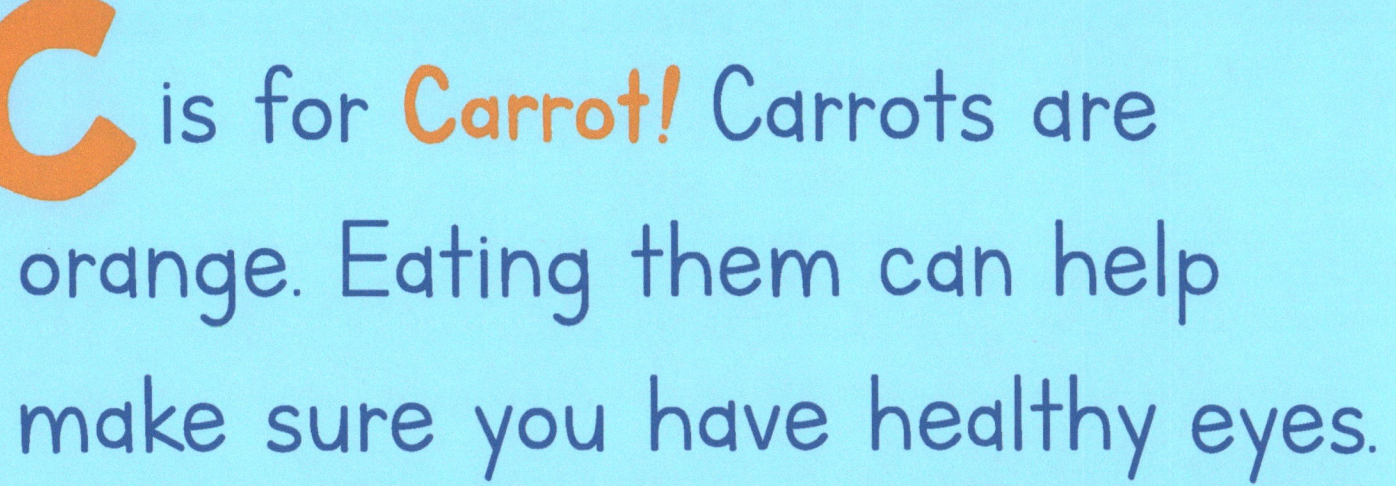

D is for **Date!** Dates are red and brown. Eating them can give your body a BOOST of energy.

E is for Eggplant! Eggplant is purple. Eating it helps keep your bones and body strong.

F is for Fruit! Fruits come in all different colours. Eating them all will help your body stay healthy.

G is for **Grapes!** Grapes are red, green and purple too. Eating them helps your heart stay healthy.

H is for Healthy! Eating all your fruits and vegetables will help your body stay healthy for life!

I is for Ice Cream Bean! Ice Cream Beans are green and eating them can help cure a headache.

J is for **Jack Fruit!** Jack Fruit is yellow and green. Since it has a lot of vitamins and minerals, eating it can help keep your body feeling good.

K is for Kiwi! Kiwi has brown skin, but is green on the inside. Eating it can help you sleep better at night.

L is for Lettuce! Lettuce is usually green but can come in red! Eating it can help your body stay hydrated.

M is for **Mushroom!** Mushrooms are white and brown in colour. Eating them gives your body a boost of Vitamin D.

N is for Nectarine! Nectarines are reddish yellow. Eating them can help keep your skin healthy.

O is for Orange! Oranges are orange. Eating them can help keep your body from getting sick.

P is for **Pineapple!** Pineapple is green and brown on the outside, but yellow on the inside. Eating it can help fix a stuffy nose.

Q is for Quince! Quinces are yellow. Eating it can help keep your hair healthy!

R is for Raspberry! Raspberries are red. Eating them can help your memory improve.

S is for Spinach! Spinach is green. Eating it can help you reduce stress.

T is for **Tomato!** Tomatoes are red. Eating them helps you maintain a healthy weight.

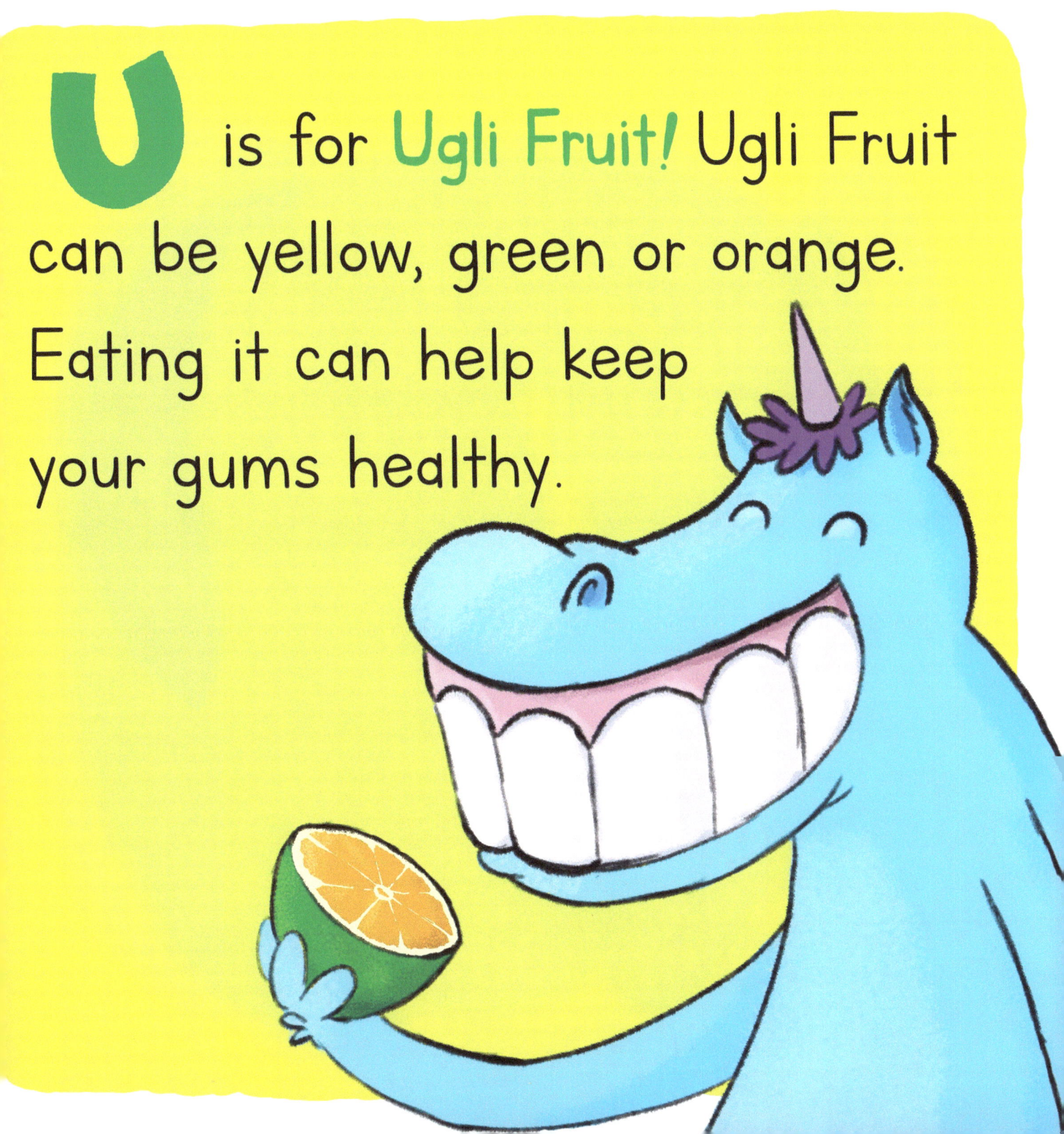

U is for Ugli Fruit! Ugli Fruit can be yellow, green or orange. Eating it can help keep your gums healthy.

V is for Vegetables!

Vegetables come in all different colours. Eating them will give your body lots of vitamins and nutrients.

W is for **Watermelon!**

Watermelons are green. Eating them can help reduce pain in your muscles.

X is for **X-Ray!** X-Rays help the doctor see how healthy your body is by eating all your fruits and vegetables.

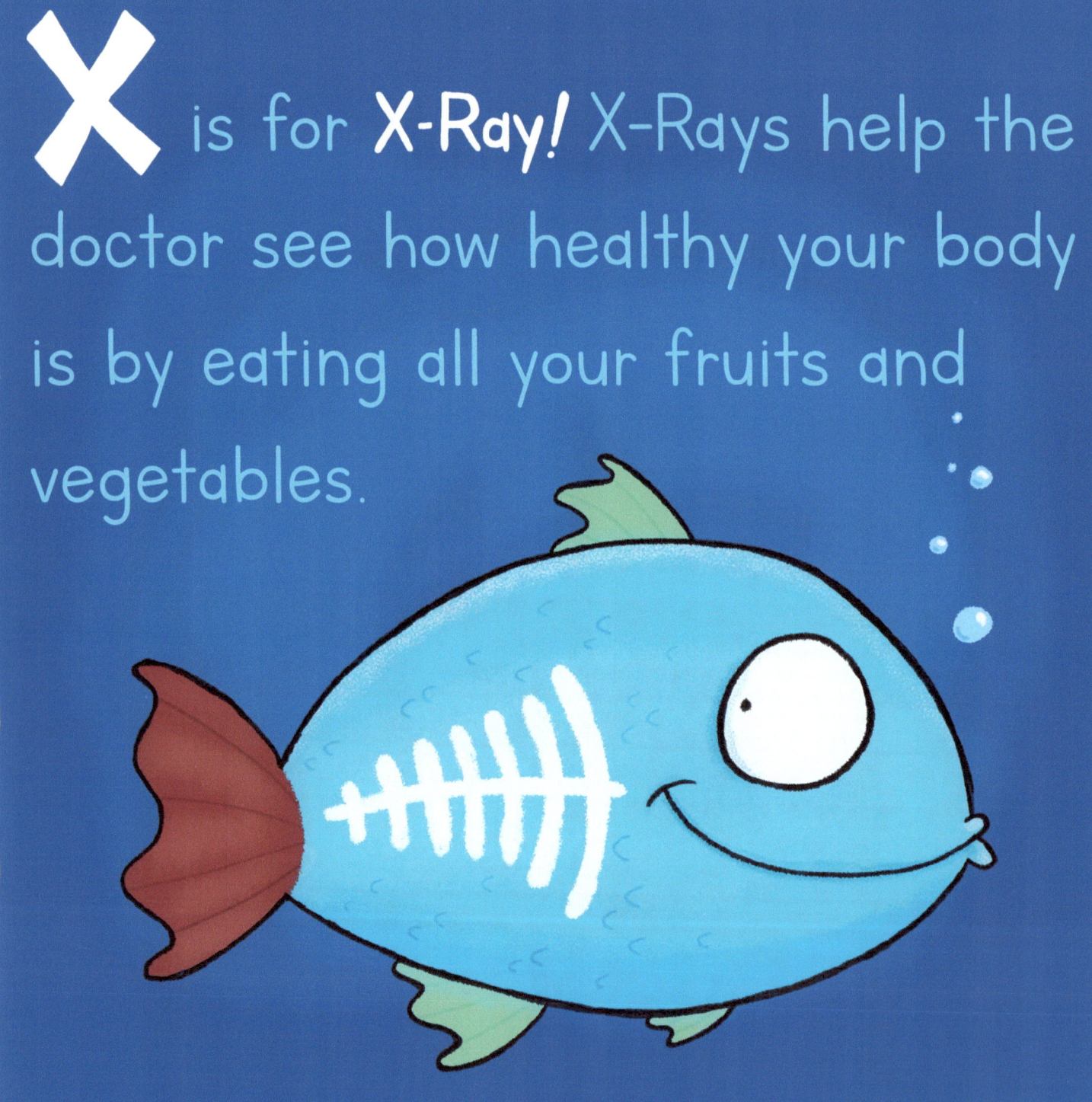

Y is for Yams! Yams can be white, red or even purple. Eating yams can help your body fight types of diseases.

Z is for Zucchini! Zucchinis are green. Eating them can help protect your skin from the sun.

A healthy diet is worth saying again!

CAN YOU NAME ALL THESE
FRUITS AND VEGETABLES

and by the way...

there are **MORE** fruits and vegetables to learn!

THE END

www.ingramcontent.com/pod-product-compliance
Lightning Source LLC
Chambersburg PA
CBHW041606120626
46551CB00002B/332